Leon's Story

Leon's Story

LEON WALTER TILLAGE

Collage art by
SUSAN L. ROTH

SQUARE
FISH

Farrar Straus Giroux
New York

To Leon Shawn Tillage and Alana Leah Roth
—Leon Walter Tillage

To Ethal Mae Tillage and Eva T. Laufer
—Susan L. Roth

SQUARE
FISH

An Imprint of Macmillan

Library of Congress Cataloging-in-Publication Data
Tillage, Leon, 1936–

Leon's story / Leon Tillage, with pictures by Susan L. Roth.

p.   cm.

Summary: The son of a North Carolina sharecropper recalls the hard times faced
by his family and other African Americans in the first half of the twentieth century
and the changes that the civil rights movement helped bring about.

ISBN 978-0-374-44330-6

1. Tillage, Leon, 1936–   —Childhood and youth—Juvenile literature. 2. Afro-Americans—North
Carolina—Fuquay-Varina—Biography—Juvenile literature. 3. North Carolina—Race relations—
Juvenile literature. 4. Civil rights movements—North Carolina—History—20th century—Juvenile
literature. 5. Fuquay-Varina (N.C.)—Biography—Juvenile literature.
6. Tillage, Leon, 1936–   [1. Afro-Americans—Biography. 2. North Carolina—Race relations.
3. Civil rights movements—History.] I. Roth, Susan L., ill. II. Title.

F264.F86T55 1997   575.6'55—dc20   [B]   96-43544

Originally published in the United States by Farrar Straus Giroux
First Square Fish Edition: September 2012
Square Fish logo designed by Filomena Tuosto
mackids.com

19 21 23 25 24 22 20

AR: 4.9 / F&P: T / LEXILE: 970L

Leon's Story

Leon

My name is Leon Walter Tillage. I was born on January 19, 1936. I have eight brothers and sisters, and I am second to the oldest. When we were growing up, we lived near Fuquay, a small Jim Crow town right outside Raleigh, the capital of North Carolina.

I remember that as a young boy I used to look in the mirror and I would curse my color, my blackness. But in those days they didn't call you "black." They didn't say "minority." They called us "colored" or "nigger."

3

Sharecropping

We lived on a farm owned by Mr. Johnson. He had lots of acres and grew lots of different crops—corn, tobacco, cotton, alfalfa, wheat, and sometimes sugarcane. It was mostly cotton and tobacco, though, because in those days those were the number one crops.

My father was a sharecropper, which means he had to share half of everything he had with Mr. Johnson. So, let's say Mr. Johnson gave my father ten acres of tobacco, ten

acres of alfalfa, ten acres of corn—whatever—
to work. Then, at the end of the year, when it
came time to sell the crops and settle up, Mr.
Johnson would get five acres of each crop and
my father would get the other five.

Maybe it sounds good, but the problem
was my father had to pay Mr. Johnson for
supplies and such, and he had purchased the
food we'd needed to live on for the past year
on credit from the corner store. So out of his
half he needed to pay off those debts.

You see, Mr. Johnson had arranged it with
the man at the corner store that we could
buy there. He'd gone to the store and said
this man or boy works for me, and I want him
to be able to get whatever he wants to eat.
You couldn't get beer or something like that,
just food. Anyway, this made Mr. Johnson re-
sponsible, so when it was time for him to give
you your money, he would first take you past
the store and you'd pay that bill. And if the
debt at the store was bigger than the money

we got from our share of the crops, Mr. Johnson would pay off the rest of the debt and you'd owe him even more.

At the end of the year, when settle-up time came, Mr. Johnson would take our crops to market. We'd settle our debts. Then Mr. Johnson would say to my father, "Well, Ivory, you almost got out of debt that time. I think next year you'll make it." And because my father had no education and couldn't read, he'd take Mr. Johnson's word for it. And because he didn't have anything but the two things he was, religious and honest, he didn't question it or try to cheat.

And that's why my grandfather also lived with us on Mr. Johnson's farm. Because once you got on a farm you could work a lifetime and never get out of debt. It wasn't usually a lot of money you owed, because when you're sharecropping like that, they just take the money off the top. It could maybe be a hundred dollars or so, but that hundred dollars seemed like a thousand—it was enough to keep you on the farm.

So that's why in those days they stayed on the farm. And when something happened to you, your children would stay on the farm because they needed to pay off their parents' debt. It was a traditional thing.

My father and grandfather and relatives, uncles and aunts, most of them, worked on those farms because they didn't have any education. They didn't see the need to have an education because even if they had an education, what kind of job could they get? They couldn't work in a bank, they couldn't work in a store. All because of their color. So they didn't see the need for education. And that was one of the ways that white men kept black men down: by not educating them. If they kept you uneducated, you weren't qualified to do anything but work on the farm. That was the only thing that my father and them were qualified to do.

Home

I remember that when we worked for Mr. Johnson, we lived in an old cruddy house in the woods behind what we called the big house. There were three or four other families on that farm, and each family pulled a share. It was like a plantation. You didn't live beside the road, you lived behind the big house—most of our houses were back down in the woods. We didn't have running water, or electric lights, and we had to see at night by lantern light. We didn't have a bathroom, just an outdoor toilet. There were five rooms: a kitchen, a pantry where you kept your pots and pans, a room for my father and mother, a room for the girls, and a room for the boys. We had a wood stove, and on the side of it they had a place you could put water, so when the stove would get hot, the water would get hot, too. Sometimes we cooked a few things in the fireplace.

My mother did a lot of cooking for the Johnsons. She would fix dinner for them. Now, the thing that's quite comical: the liquid stuff that came from the collard greens and the greens she was cooking—we called it pot likker—they'd give it to her to bring home. What would happen, she would get home, make corn bread, and dumplings, and she would turn the pot likker into a soup like. And the amazing thing was the white people couldn't understand why we was so much healthier and bigger than their kids. But we found out later on in life, when you boil the greens and cook the greens, the vitamins went down into the juice, so we got the best part.

My parents were very strict. There was a lot of boys in our family, and you know how boys do every once in a while, they get in arguments. But my parents didn't allow no fighting among the children. Another thing they was very strict on: you had to be respectful. It didn't matter who it was or what color they were—it was always "Yes, ma'am" and "Yes, sir."

My family was very close. My parents was real religious, and I remember before we'd go to bed at night, we'd all get together and get on our knees, and you'd have to say your prayers. And before you ate you had to say a blessing. There was no way you'd sit down and eat without blessing the food.

We were in church every Sunday, and most of the time my parents took dinner and stuff, so we were practically in church all day. My parents would spread the dinner out on the lawn and everybody would chip in and just sit down and eat and have a good time, and the kids would run and play. And then after we ate, the reverend would call us back into church, and then he was praying again and we had to stay there.

When I was young, my grandmother—my mother's mother—was like some eighty years of age. I can slightly remember her sitting on a chair and telling us about her mother. She could remember when she was a little girl; she could remember slavery. And *her* mother was a slave. She used to tell us about cooking, washing, how they made what they call lye soap, and typical work round the farm. She had little chores she had to do—get eggs from the henhouse and stuff like that. We didn't have a television or radio and that was one of our recreation times, sitting around the fireplace after dinner and listening to the elder people, my grandfather and grandmother.

In those days, Christmas also brought people together. Not only that—white and black would meet up. You could go to a white person's house and they would give you things. It was a time of giving and rejoicing. We kids just could not wait for it.

Christmas Day was a spiritual day—that was the day you'd go to church. The day after Christmas and Christmas Eve, that was the fun time. But Christmas we were mostly in church all day. And then Santa Claus would come Christmas night. We would get some little toy. I would always get a harmonica, some cheap little harmonica; my sisters and brothers would get little dolls, rag dolls, cheap stuff, but to us it was a precious gift because we had no toys.

We used to go to bed early Christmas night and get up before day, and under the

Christmas tree we'd have presents and we'd have fruit and stuff like that in shoe boxes, and we were the happiest kids in the world. I remember some kids didn't get anything, and the thing about it, they would start coming around to visit you because they wanted to play with your toys, so what would happen is your parents would make you put up your toys while they were there because sometimes kids can be destructive and jealous because they don't have anything, and we would be upset because our parents wouldn't let us play with our toys, and we would always try to figure out a way to get our company to go away.

The two things that would bring everybody together, white and colored, was Christmas or a death in the family. If someone would die in the family, people would come to that family's home and sit up all night long, oh, for about two or three days or something like that. You'd be surprised, a lot of the white people would come and bring food and even bring clothes in for the family. And it would work the other way around: if some white person would die, we would go and do the same thing, and that was just the way it was. It shows how you can come together.

Helping Out

Everybody had a job to do on the farm—the boys had a job to do, the girls had a job to do—and after school we had chores to do. During the summer I would leave with my father early in the morning and work on the farm. What happened in a deal like that was we didn't get paid—we was helping out my father, 'cause we had tobacco and stuff like that. If we did do something for Mr. Johnson on the farm, he would give us seventy-five cents or something like that and we would be very happy. He would say, "I want the boys to go out and pull some weeds," or, "I want the boys to do this for me," and we would love to do that because that was the only change we could get, and that way we could go to the movies or go downtown and buy some sodas or stuff like that. But as far as my father giving us something extra for helping him out, the poor guy didn't have anything to give us. You know, he fed us and stuff like that.

In those days, school was out at roughly two. We would come straight home because we had stuff to do. Now, you must realize in those days you also had to chop wood and get in water for the night. They didn't tell you you had to do these things, you just did them. Even if we had to go out and help shuck some corn or whatever, we would always get back home in time to chop up some wood because in those days we burned wood in the fireplace and burned wood in the stove. I think one of the reasons we didn't get into trouble is we didn't have time. We had chores, we had things to do at all times, and we didn't have too much free time on our hands.

In the summer my father would be harvesting tobacco. He'd hook the mule to the plow, and one of the jobs we did for him was to walk behind with a stick, and what would happen is, if my father happened to accidentally throw some dirt over the tobacco, we would take the stick and flip the tobacco up—the dirt would smother it, you see. So we walked behind the plow to uncover it.

While we kids worked in the hot summertime, we wondered why Mr. Johnson's kids never worked. He had children that were approximately our age and a little older, and they would stay up under the pecan tree and drink lemonade while everybody else's kids were out there working. And we kids couldn't understand why we worked all the time and then at the end of the year we didn't have anything. My father wasn't even able to buy us decent clothes or anything like that. Mr. Johnson would advance him a hundred dollars to go buy us clothes, but of course that meant that he was a hundred dollars more in debt for the next year. And there was nothing my father could do about it.

We kids wanted to know why we had to live in an old broken-down house. Why we had to walk around with no new shoes. Why we couldn't have a pretty car like Mr. Johnson and them. Once I went to Mr. Johnson's house and saw his son Harold's room. Harold was about my age. I looked at all the beautiful furniture and saw how beautiful it was in the house and everything, and I couldn't figure out why we didn't have some of these nice things. We knew somewhere something was wrong, but we just couldn't figure out what to do about it. Why in America we had to be second best. Our parents would only say, "Well, that's the way it's intended, that's the way it's supposed to be. You'll never equal up to the whites."

Our parents' attitudes were different in those days. If my son asked me something now, I would try to explain things to him to my best ability, but in those days you did not question your parents. They was very strict and they would give you a quick answer and that was it. You didn't feel bad about it, you just didn't ask them anymore, and that was the way it was.

School

I started school when I was six. You got
to school when you could because you had
things to do around the house before you left
in the morning. In the springtime you didn't
go as often because you had to help take care
of the crops. Education didn't mean too much
to my father; the way they looked at it in
those days was, you were colored, so all you
needed to learn was how to read your name,
write your name, stuff like that, but why sit
in school? You'll never get a job in the bank,

or you'll never get a job down in the drug-store, so it was a waste of time to him. My mother had a little different opinion about it. She wanted us to read. My brother James and I taught my mother how to read and write. My father, we finally did teach him how to write his name, how to sign things, but he wasn't interested in education. He did love to hear us read; we'd read the Bible or something to him.

As I was getting older, I got a little education and I could better myself, you know, because I could read and write. And later, when I worked in different places, once they knew I could read and write, they would give me a little more responsibility. So instead of being the one unloading the trucks, they would give me a notebook where I'd write down what was being unloaded and the numbers and all. It meant I could get a little better job.

• • •

The first school I went to was Providence School. It was in a big house. They had knocked down all the walls and made three rooms out of it. There weren't any grades. You just went to school and basically all they taught you was your ABC's and your times tables. You would read; we had some books that we had gotten from the white school which were just reading books. That was the type of education we were getting at that early age.

My first teacher was my cousin, and she graduated high school in New York, but she came back South, and they gave her a job teaching us at Providence. Now the point is she had never been to college. But she was teaching us the basics: how to spell your name, your times tables, and just how to read in general. But later, when we went to high school in Fuquay, then the teachers came from Raleigh, from Shaw University.

We lived about four miles from the school

in Providence, and we had to walk every day. Some of the kids lived even farther out than we did, and they walked, too. The white kids had a school bus they rode in. And when we got to school in the mornings we had to go out in the woods in the freezing cold and chop wood. We used to bring the wood in and start the fire in the big old potbelly heater. We had to go out and draw water up out of the well. We had to put cardboard in some of the windows because most of the time they were broken. My mother and the rest of the mothers would give us a can of beans or white potatoes or something to take because that was the way we ate our lunch. The teacher had a huge cooking pot that she would put on the potbelly heater and she would mix all this stuff up. It was amazing how sometimes some of the kids couldn't bring anything, but the teachers would still make enough so they would get something to eat, too. We used to—just to show you the cruelty in children at that time—tease the kids that didn't have anything to bring, and many a time I've regretted it. Basically, it was the same kids and most of them came from large families; some people had ten, eleven, twelve, fourteen kids, and it was hard.

We brought our own tin cups and spoons and left them there. We used to buy peaches in those cups, they were nice-size cups, and that's mostly what everybody used. After we ate everything up, we'd put water in the pot, put it back on the heater, and when the water got hot, we'd wash our own cups out. Each kid washed their own stuff, and the teacher would inspect it.

That was the way we ate because we didn't have no kitchen or nothing like that at the school. The white kids had all that stuff. They had a big beautiful building. They had steam heat. They had a kitchen, a school bus, and everything.

When we left school for the day and

started walking home, we'd keep looking back until we saw the white kids' school bus. If we saw that bus coming, we would automatically take off and start running, looking for someplace to hide. If the bus driver stopped the bus when he got to where we were, we knew we were really in trouble. That meant the bigger boys and girls would get out of the bus and start calling us names. They would pick up stones and start throwing them at us. The larger black kids would act like decoys. They would get hit to keep the little children from getting hit. You would protect your little sister or brother or any little kid. It didn't make any difference if they were related or not, you didn't want them to get hurt. And the white kids didn't care who they hit, just as long as they hit someone. So what you would do was when they were throwing stones at you, you would start screaming and hollering and begging. They liked that, and most of the time they would let up on you. So long as they hit somebody, they were happy and you could hear them bragging, saying, "Hey, did you see me hit that one? Boy, I really hit him or her." Then they would go run and jump back in the bus and they would take off.

But I also remember a white man named Mr. Clark. He had a big white horse, and sometimes he would come down to the school when we'd get out and he would walk with us, him and his horse. When he would see the bus coming, he would tell us, "Don't run, don't run, they're not going to bother you." He was a good man, he was a religious man. And he was right—they wouldn't bother us if he was there.

Sometimes when we got hit, we would run to his house and have a knot on our head or be bleeding or something, and his wife would come out and help us. Her name was Miss Janie. She would come out and say, "It's a shame how they do this and they shouldn't do you young-uns like that." She'd make us feel better. Sometimes she'd have cookies and stuff like that she would give to us.

I think mostly all the blacks in that vicinity loved the Clarks. They treated us like people. And when you did some work on their farm, she would fix food and you would eat at their table, which was very amazing in those times. You know, we were used to eating out under the tree, but she would call you in the house. And I remember Mr. Clark used to sit at the end of the table and say a prayer. And we'd sit there and eat. And when you got through eating, you'd get up and go back to work.

Now, the white kids didn't bother us every day. Sometimes they would come past and just call us names and keep going. And sometimes the bus driver would just tease us. He'd stop the bus, we'd see the red light come on, and we'd all start running, and it was real funny to them, real comical. But they didn't do that every day.

The white people would teach their kids that black people had no feelings. They didn't have no soul, it didn't matter what you did to them, you couldn't hurt their feelings because they didn't have feelings. You could hit them or whatever, and you couldn't hurt them. And this is why they treated us like they did— they actually thought this.

Later we took a bus to Fuquay High School, and that was a step up. We were very happy because they built a new school, and the teachers came from Raleigh and we had good books and steam heat, we didn't have to go out in the woods and get wood. We had a cafeteria, and I remember they would give you your food for fifteen cents, but that fifteen cents could seem like fifteen dollars. Sometimes Mr. Johnson would give us lunch money when we'd walk past his house in the morning to get the bus. He would come out and say to us, have you got money for lunch? We'd tell him whether we did or didn't, and me being the oldest, he would like give me a dollar, and I would pay for the rest of my brothers' and sisters' lunches. We were very proud of our school. It even had a janitor who fired the furnace and did odds-and-ends work around there for us.

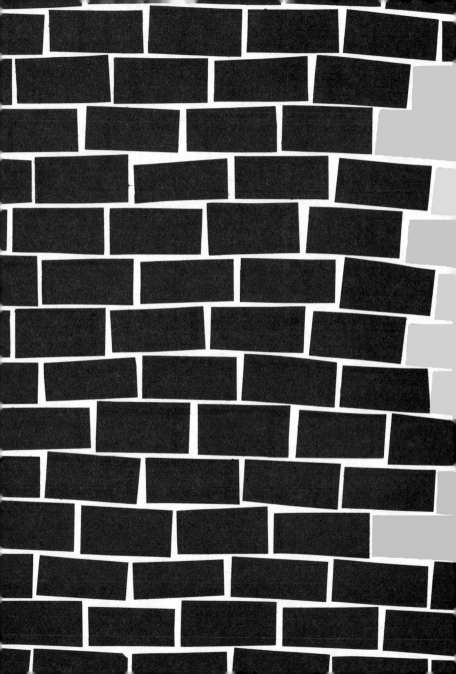

White Only

Some Saturday nights we used to go to the movies in our little town because in those days we didn't have television, we didn't even have electric lights. So going to the movies was a big thing. I remember my father and I went to see *Gone With the Wind*, but I think that was the first time and the last time we went to the movies together. He liked Clark Gable. But I mostly went with my friends. The reason we loved to go to the movies were the Westerns. We had Gene Autry,

Roy Rogers; they were heroes in those days.

If you did something wrong, my dad would say, "You won't go to the movies if you don't straighten up," or something like that. I'd rather for him to take a leather strap to me than say I couldn't go to the movies, because that's where most of my friends would be. That was a big thing, going to the movies.

It was fifteen cents to get in the movie, and someone would bring around popcorn, soda, and candy bars, which cost five cents. We had to sit up in the balcony. The whites sat at the bottom in what looked like nice soft chairs, and sometimes we sat on Coca-Cola crates because they couldn't fit that many chairs in the balcony. During intermission, we would jump up and run to the rear of the movie house, where there were some steps leading outside, and we'd sit on the steps until the lights went off again and the movie was going to start, because when the lights were on, the white kids would throw stuff—popcorn and things like that—up into the balcony, and you didn't want to get hit. Sometimes the owner's son would stand down front, where there was a railing about waist-high, and if anyone threw stuff into the balcony, he would throw them out. But most of the time he wouldn't be there. When we got ready to leave, we used to go to the glass door in the front of the theater and stand there and watch and wait until the white kids left. Because if you went out there when they were out there, you would get jumped. It wasn't all of them, just some troublemakers having fun. They would hide behind the building and we'd come out and then they would chase us. Now, the colored part of town wasn't too far—it was right over the track; and if they chased you and caught you before you got to that track, they had these sticks they would beat you with.

· · ·

When I was about sixteen, I'd go out and make my own money by working around on the farms and at different places, and I went out and bought my own school clothes. You'd work half a day Saturday. Then the guy would pay you, and first thing you'd do is go buy a pair of pants or pair of shoes or something like that, but it wasn't no routine. There wasn't much money, but you could get a pair of pants for under two dollars.

We used to go into Raleigh to a big store. And as usual, we had to go in the back door, marked COLORED. If I saw a pair of pants I wanted, I walked up and stood there and looked at the pants, and as soon as somebody felt like coming to wait on me, I'd give them a little smile and say, "I'd like to buy these pants please, sir or ma'am." If I was standing there waiting for a salesperson and a white person walked up, I automatically stepped back and stood there with a smile on my face. Now, that person would look through the clothes and I'd just wait there. So finally the person who worked in the store would come over to the white person and say to him, "Is he bothering you? Do you mind him standing here? Do you want me to put him out of the store?" If that person was nice, they would say, "No, he isn't bothering me, it's okay." But if the person said, "Yes, I don't want him here watching me," the salesperson would automatically tell you to get out of the store. That was the way it was. You couldn't try on the clothes you wanted. You'd mostly know your size. There was one place you could; it was a Jewish store near my house, and they would let you try on shoes and stuff like that, but that was the only place.

There was also a five-and-dime. They had twinkling things, like women's earrings and stuff like that, belts for men and tiepins. But they had a long counter that went from one end to the other end, and they would have places for the white people to sit and eat at the counter and then they had a long rope, and hanging from the rope were these little signs that said WHITE ONLY. Well, we couldn't understand why they would do that because no black person would try to sit on the stools, no way. But when it was hot out, I used to walk on the other side of the rope real slowly, and I would look for a young man about my age. And I would look at him and smile, and if he looked back at me and smiled, I would whisper, "Buy me a soda." He would get up and stand beside the rope and I handed him the money, and when he came back he gave me the soda and I thanked him and got out of the store as fast as I could, because if I got caught drinking that soda in the store I would be in trouble. My mother and them, they used to think we was crazy-like, you know, they didn't understand why we would try to buck the system. They stayed in their place, and that's why they got along good. But for us it was bucking the system, it was a dare. I mean, you could buy soda anywhere; out on the streets they had pushcarts, but it wasn't like the soda that you could get from where you weren't supposed to get it. The soda didn't taste no different from any other soda, it was just where you got it from.

In those days they had what they called Tastee-Freez alongside the roads our way, and you would walk up and they would have WHITE ONLY and then they had COLORED with an arrow pointing to the rear of the building. You would go in back of the building and they had a window they would open up. Now, when you went back there, you just stood there and waited. You didn't go back there and tap on the window; you didn't go back there and yell at the guy to come and wait on you or anything like that. You just stood there. The guy would see you. He may not be doing anything, he might be reading the paper or whatever. But you stood there if you wanted to get waited on until he got ready and felt like coming back there. When he did wait on me, the first thing he would say is "What do you want?" and if I had a hat on I would take it off and with a big beautiful smile I would say, "Give me a hot dog, please, sir." And he would go get the hot dog, but not before I'd put money down on the windowsill so I didn't touch him when I handed him the money. Then he would pick the money up and go get the hot dog if he felt like it. If he didn't feel like it, he didn't. That was the way it was, and you just left.

I remember that you would go to the bus station to catch the bus and they would have a sign there for coloreds pointing to the rear.

You'd go around to the back of the bus station, and that's where you would go in and you would sit down. Sometimes soldier boys would come in, the white soldiers, and if they were rowdy they'd put them out of the white station, and they'd come around to the black side and drink their beer and carry on and jump up on the chairs and act like idiots. And there was nothing nobody could do about it. Most of the black people, like the older ones, would get up and go on the outside, but nobody would bother with the soldiers, nobody would say anything to them.

Klansmen

In those days, blacks didn't have any voice at all, and there was no such thing as taking the white man to court. You couldn't vote; you weren't even considered a citizen. We were afraid to approach certain white men in the wrong way because of the Ku Klux Klan. We wasn't afraid of all whites, just certain ones, because the Klansmen were very dangerous people. I mean they could hurt you or kill you for no reason at all, and there was nothing done about it.

I was afraid to walk the road at night because of the Klansmen. It was all dirt roads in those days. If I was walking down a road at night, I would constantly be looking behind me. If a car came, I automatically jumped down the embankment and hid in the ditch, or if it was a wooded area, I would run out in the woods and lay down and be real quiet, because if they caught me, they'd beat me up and hurt me, and they called it having fun. To them it was fun.

If you were hidden and they saw you, they would yell at you and try and get you to come to the car by saying they weren't going to bother you. Or they would slam the car door like they were gone and then drive off and leave two or three of them standing there, and if you came out of the bushes or whatever, they would jump on you and beat you up. We used to walk the railroad track or walk the footpath at night in the woods at the edge of the fields so we wouldn't be seen out there in the open. If you did, you would really regret it.

Sometimes the Klansmen rode horses or walked. They carried a cross with them. They would burn the crosses in people's yards. We would go into the little town of Fuquay, and the word was passed around that you had better be careful tonight because the Klansmen were going to be riding. And we wouldn't know whose house they were coming to or what they were going to do, but we heard that the Klansmen were coming somewhere tonight.

Sometimes Mr. Johnson would say to my father, like on a Saturday night, "You all better lay in tonight, you better be careful, I heard the Klansmen is gonna be riding." Now, he was a good guy, and he'd probably said to the Klansmen, "Just give 'em a scare." The whites, they wanted to keep us home so we wouldn't meet up somewhere. Now, if you had done something wrong to any white person, then you wasn't protected, and the Klansmen would beat you. The point is, if you did what you was supposed to do, walked the chalk line, was a good guy, no problems, they would just ride through, let you know they still here, and frighten you.

Those nights my father would climb the ladder and go up on top of the house and sit beside the chimney, and I'd climb the ladder, too, and take him coffee, and sometimes my grandfather would sit up there with him. They would be watching for the Klansmen. When the Klansmen came, my father would pound on the roof three times. Nobody was in bed but the young-uns. We sat up with the lights out to wait and see if the Klansmen came. If they came, we used to take off—my father and mother and grandfather and us kids—everybody had a hiding place that we knew where to go, because we lived in the woods anyway, and we would go hide until the Klansmen left.

That was the type of life we lived in those days. But it was all natural, it was all part of survival. Most of the time it wasn't even discussed. You see, our parents were real religious, and they felt as though God was going to take care of them. Anything that happened in the neighborhood by one of the whites, they didn't hold that against them, they wasn't angry about it. They used to pray, and they would say, "God's gonna punish him." See, to them—they were superstitious-like— there was a few things that happened to some white people, and they would say, "See?" I remember this one man that was mean to his tenants, he was riding his horse and hit a limb and it killed him, and they said God punished him. They wasn't interested in participating in marches and stuff like that; they felt like

Moses was gonna lead the blacks out of bondage like he did the Jewish people. They was thinking—don't forget, we're dealing with people here who are uneducated, real religious, and they believed everything—the only thing they could believe in was God, they prayed about every little thing that went wrong. They figured He was going to send somebody from heaven. Thank God they had that to hold on to.

I've had people ask me, "Why didn't you call the police or why didn't you get the police?" We were afraid of the police because a lot of them were Klansmen. We didn't call them police in those days. They were called either a sheriff or a constable. There was this one constable who had been an amateur boxer. He would lock up a black person and he would put gloves on them and practice on them. And there was one boy, Scott, that he put gloves on, and he hit that boy and he killed him. Scott's brother went up there to check on him and try and get him out, and he found out his brother was dead. He approached the constable to see what happened, and the constable killed him, too. Both brothers in one night. It was never, never investigated or nothing. He had beat up people and knocked people's teeth out and everything, and nothing was never done or investigated or nothing.

Fifteenth Birthday

When I was around fourteen, we'd worked off our debt to Mr. Johnson and moved off his farm to Mr. Tompkins's farm, where we rented a house. Mr. Tompkins was a black guy who had inherited his land from his father or somebody. It wasn't a huge farm, like the Johnson farm with acres and acres and acres. I think he had something like twenty-five or thirty acres, but in those days for a black man that was amazing.

We didn't sharecrop on Mr. Tompkins's

farm, it wasn't large enough. We just worked for him on his farm and he paid us. After a while my father decided that we should go back to Johnson's farm, that we would do better there, but just before we moved, my father was killed.

It was my fifteenth birthday. My father and mother left the house to go to Fuquay to get me a little gift, as they usually did. Some white boys came past our house in a car and they were screaming and hollering, all drunk up, and we kids could see my father and mother walking. I remember before the car got to my father. I remember seeing my father and mother take off and start running. They were trying to make it to the next house, and they took off running. I remember seeing my father as the car was coming at him. I remember seeing my father shove my mother down a deep embankment. I saw it clearly. By that time the car hit him and knocked him down. Us kids, we saw all this happen. And the car went to the next driveway and turned around.

I watched my father trying to get up, but evidently his hip or his leg was broken, one of the two or both was broken, because they'd hit him on the side and he couldn't stand up. The car came back and pulled over to where my father was and the driver ran completely over him, as though he was running over a dog or something. And my father got caught underneath the car and they drug him almost back up to the house where we were living. My brothers and sisters, we were all looking at this. And the boys in the car jumped out and looked underneath and saw that my father was stuck underneath it. They pulled him out. Then they jumped in the car and took off. We came out our front door and they yelled at us and threw beer cans at us. We ran down there.

I was the first one to my father, but he was dead. He was all busted up, big hole in his head. He was dead. I looked to where my mother was laying down in the embankment. She was knocked out. She didn't even know what happened.

The next morning, this boy, the driver, and his father came up to our house. We knew who they were. They had a big farm and they were a very prominent family. They also ran a car place, they were what we used to call parking lot dealers. They were wealthy people. This boy and his father went to see my mother, who was in bed because she was hurt bad and she was upset. The man said to my mother, "Well, I'm sorry what happened. But you know how it is, boys will be boys. My wife told me to give you a hundred dollars. I don't know. A hundred dollars is a lot of money, but she told me to give it to you and this will help with the funeral bill." And then he turned around to his son and said, "Say you're sorry. Tell her you're sorry you ran over her husband." But the boy wouldn't open his mouth. He just turned around and walked out of the house. So the father said, "Well, I apologize for him. I'm sorry, but I hope you can get along without your husband, and you'll just have to face the facts that these things happen."

And that was all that was done about it. A sheriff never came to the house, nobody investigated it, nothing. They didn't do anything, and we didn't hear any more about it. But that wasn't the first time things like that happened. I mean, people had gotten run over and people had got hit by cars and crippled by cars, and there was never nothing done.

My mother finally did later on go to court, in Raleigh, but they never did anything about it, they just threw it right out of court. She had an appointed lawyer because she didn't have any money to pay for a lawyer, but I can't remember really if he did anything. They just wanted to be able to say, later on down the road, that we did get our day in court. Now it would be different, but in those days it didn't matter what you felt about the crime, because what could you do about it? It's not that we accepted my father's death, we cared, but we just minded our own business and stayed out of the spotlight because nothing was going to be done about it anyway.

Mr. Johnson was very good to us when my father was killed. He'd known my father all his life, and my father's father worked with him. He went to the funeral and he bought us all suits to wear to the funeral. I think, quite frankly, these were our first suits.

And so we moved back to Mr. Johnson's farm. It wasn't the old farm. Mr. Johnson had bought another farm, a modern farm. So the house where we went back to when we left Tompkins's farm, it still didn't have a bathroom in it, we had well water on the outside, but it had electric lights and it was a nice, tight house. We liked the place and we lived and worked there until Mr. Johnson got sick and died. After that, we didn't get along with his sons, the younger ones, because they started fighting over the farm and everything, so we moved to another farm—the Deans'.

Anyway, it was a different relationship when we returned to Mr. Johnson's because the times were a little different. I mean, you didn't make a lot of money, but you would make more then than before because kids were now educated some. Like when my mother would go to Mr. Johnson to get money, I'd write down what he wrote down. Or, for instance, when we needed fertilizer or something like that, I would go with him to get fertilizer, and I'd write down the price of fertilizer, and he would write it down, too, and this way we kept the same books. But years before then you couldn't do that, it was considered an insult.

71

Odd Jobs

Whenever I could, I worked odd jobs trying to make some extra money. That's the way we did it. If a friend of mine was working somewhere, he would say, "Hey, they're paying a quarter over here . . . fifteen cents more here . . ." In other words, it was survival. You just worked wherever you could work to get some more money so you could buy some pants or something. My mother did what she could do, but we had to pitch in. That was all that mattered. We knew what to do with our little change, even just eat it up.

Once I was working at the tobacco market. I worked there after school and at night helping to unload the trucks and work around the warehouse in general.

I was standing in the aisle and two guys and a little boy came up behind me. I didn't see them. The little boy touched me on my leg and said, "Pardon me, I want to get past." I stepped over to one side. The father stopped the little boy right there in his tracks and said, "What did you say to him?" And the little boy just looked at him. He didn't know what was going on, and the father said, "I said, what did you say to him?" And the little boy said, "I said pardon me?" And his father slapped him in the face and told him, "You never do that. You never in your life tell a nigger pardon. You kick him if he is in your way." He told the little boy to kick me. And the little boy kicked me right on the shinbone. In fact he kicked me twice. He started walking off and looked back at me with his blue eyes and he had a sad look on his face as though he was sorry. I'll never forget the look on that kid's face as long as I live.

They had two water fountains at the market. One had a sign on it for whites and one for coloreds, the same thing as the bathrooms. There was this older black man who couldn't read. He must have gotten the fountains mixed up. Anyway, he drank some water from the white fountain and a white guy saw him. The white guy jumped off his truck with a tobacco stick—that was a wooden pole that was about six feet long and about one inch in diameter, and that's what we would hang our tobacco on—and he went over there and he hit that old man—and that old man was still drinking water—and he hit that old man across the head and he broke that tobacco stick over that man's head. By that time there were about three or four more white guys jumping in, and they beat and kicked that poor man until they almost beat him to death. All because he took a drink out of the white fountain.

Another time I worked at a restaurant there in Fuquay, and I couldn't use the front door. We used to wait in the parking lot, and when the guy opened the door for us to come in and start work we had to go around to the back door, while the white employees used the front door. We couldn't work out front or anything like that. We had to work in the kitchen and in the rear. And even though we cleaned the bathrooms before the customers came, we still better not get caught using one of those bathrooms or we were in trouble. If, after they'd closed and everybody had left, you needed to take the trash out the front, you could run out the front door—but as far as coming to work, no, you couldn't do that.

• • •

One job I had was on the outskirts of Raleigh, and I had to catch the bus to get there. In those days when you caught the bus, you had to get on twice. You would get on the bus and pay, but you could not walk through the white section. You had to get off the bus and come around and get on through the side door. Now, the bus had a white line in the center of it, and you could not cross that line. I don't care how many people was in the rear of the bus, if it wasn't but one white person sitting across that line, you still couldn't cross that line. When the white section filled up, the white people would get on the bus and come back across the line and you could not sit down. Before they sat down, some of the white people would take out their handkerchiefs and spread them out on the seat and sit down on them. If a lot of white people kept getting on, and they filled up the back of the bus, the driver would stop and put you off the bus. They wouldn't give you your money back or nothing. They would just say, "Okay, off you go. You, you, you, and you, get off." And you would have to get off the bus, and sometimes you'd have to start running because you didn't want to be late for work.

I worked for a white man who drank a lot of beer. This was a guy who hauled pulpwood and needed help sawing and loading his truck. One Saturday afternoon we pulled up at this beer tavern, and he parked under a shady tree right along the road. I couldn't go in with him, so I sat in the pickup truck waiting for him. I was sitting there for a while when all of a sudden I looked up and saw men and women coming out of the tavern. I was wondering what was going on, and then I saw that they were coming toward the pickup, and I knew something was wrong and that I was going to be the victim. So I sat there for a minute and I didn't know what to do, and then I saw this guy coming around the building with two huge dogs.

I still didn't know what to do, and I figured this was the end of my life now, because I knew they were going to sic those dogs on me. I locked the truck door. When they got to the truck, the guy that I was working for said to me, "Open that truck door, unlock it." But I wouldn't unlock the door. So he took his keys out and unlocked the door. I jumped out of the truck and jumped up on top of it. The man that had the dogs said to me, "All right, boy, run for your life. If you make it to that tree and climb the tree, I'll call the dogs off of you." I could see people pulling their money out, making bets on whether I would make it or not. Well, I didn't know what to do. I figured this was the end of my life now. What a horrible way to go. And they kept saying, "Run, run, I said run."

The man turned both dogs loose. The dogs

came and were jumping up, and one grabbed me by my heel and was trying to pull me off the truck. I was kicking at it. I will never forget it. I was holding on to the truck for dear mercy, screaming and hollering and pleading to the man to call his dogs off. I was hollering and crying and pleading to the man that I worked for to help me, help me please.

By that time, by the help of God—I have to believe it was a miracle that happened—two white guys came along, and they jammed on the brakes to their car. They jumped out, and one of them had a shotgun and he said to the guy with the dogs, "If you don't call the dogs off, I'm going to kill them." And the man called the dogs off. In the meantime, he told me to run. He said, "Take off—run." I took off and started running with my leg bleeding and everything, and I ran down the road and I didn't know which way to go, and I kept looking back because I didn't know whether they were going to catch me or chase me or what. There was a big drainpipe that ran underneath the road. I ran up in that drainpipe and lay down frightened to death. I stayed in that pipe for the rest of the afternoon, and I waited until it got dark before I came out because I was afraid and I didn't know if they were still looking for me. That was the life you had to live in those days. But I never worked for that man again.

Marching

Now, what was happening was, as our schools were getting better along about this time in the 1950s, we were learning that we weren't supposed to be living like this regardless of what our parents said. We learned that we had certain rights: freedom of speech, freedom of religion. We learned about the Constitution of the United States. We learned that all men are created equal. We knew it was time for change.

I remember that when I was in about the

eleventh grade, people started coming around to the schools, and wanted high-school students to participate in marches. These people wanted to march in Raleigh, and they would come around and talk to you about it. It wasn't like there was someone insisting, but they would explain to you about how you would go about it and what they were going to do, and it was up to you if you wanted to. They didn't have to talk too much—we were ready for a movement. Of course, we figured it would be a little violent, but we didn't know it was going to be rough as it was. Our parents would say to us, "We don't understand. Don't you know you're going to get killed for listening to these people? You're going to get beat up. What's wrong with you?" Then we would say to them, "We're getting beat up now. We're getting killed now. So I'd rather get beat up for doing something or trying to change things. I mean, why get beat up for nothing?" That's what we used to reply back to them.

Martin Luther King, Jr., went to Raleigh. He went to the capitals because that's where the governors and mayors and everybody was at. I remember he would send these representatives out to see us at the high school, and they would also go to the college in Raleigh, a black college, Shaw University. These people would come to us because there was no need to talk to our parents and people like that because they couldn't participate in the movement: first of all, because they lived on these farms, and if the white man found out that they were participating in this type of movement, they would automatically be kicked off the farm and not be able to get a job anywhere else; and second of all, the Klansmen would catch them. So the only people they would talk to were high-school students and college people.

Later, when I was a little older, we used to meet up in Raleigh in the mornings to march. We would meet up by the mayor's house. When we got there to start the march, the Klansmen would be there waiting. They marched before we marched, and they had their signs about white power and all this stuff, and the police would escort them. We couldn't understand why the police escorted them, because nobody was going to bother them.

Now, before we marched, we used to get rubber inner tubes and we would cut them up. We would take our clothes off and tie the inner tube around our bodies and around our arms. Then we'd put our regular pants back on and a big pair of coveralls or anything real loose over that. We also used to make stocking caps from cotton stockings that ladies wore, and we would take either newspaper or cotton and fold it up and put it on our heads and take these stocking caps and put them over that. The inner tubes were in case we were jumped by a dog. The paper or cotton was in case we were beaten.

When it was our time to start marching, the Klansmen and the white citizens stood on one side. We would lock arms. We would start marching, and people would start throwing things at us. They used to have human waste in paper bags. They would run up and try to throw rotten eggs in our faces. They used to urinate in milk bottles, and they would try to throw that on us. But we kept marching. We were determined and we felt we had nothing to lose. It was a good thing Martin Luther King was nonviolent, because if both sides would have been fighting and carrying weapons and stuff like that, it would have been chaos. I still believe that was the only solution, to be non-violent.

It was a heck of a feeling—to not know

whether we were going to live for the next hour or not. Because it was rumored that some of the Klansmen had guns. It was rumored that they would throw dynamite in the crowd. It was an awful feeling, too. We had police standing shoulder to shoulder. They weren't going to let us pass. And we tried to break the length of the police. They had dogs. We would start running because of those dogs. The main thing was not to fall down if you could help it. If you fell down, you could really get hurt or mauled by one of the dogs. You had to stay up on your feet.

Now, some of the police would beat on you, but they wouldn't be hitting you that hard. They was just going through the motions, and they would say, "Run, run!" Those were the good policemen.

After you got past the police, then you had the firemen with water hoses from their trucks. And believe me, that water could actually peel the skin right off of you. They would put a lot of water on the street. You would take your hands and fold them between your legs so your limbs wouldn't be flopping all about you, and you would go down with the water and let it push you wherever it would. You didn't try to fight it or nothing like that.

We would start running down the street because the police and the dogs and the Klansmen—everybody was chasing us, and we would just start running. And I remember that there were Greeks and Jewish people with businesses there. They would stand in their doorways and motion for us to run in the store. We used to run down in their basements and hide.

Sometimes there were people sitting down at the end of Fayetteville Street with cars. There were black and white people sitting in cars, and you would run and jump in a car that would take off and take you out of the city.

There was a black section in Raleigh. You would think they would have helped us if we made it to their section and we would be safe. But they would be standing with shovels, ice picks, anything to keep us out. They said we were troublemakers and they hated us. Those people worked in Raleigh, and because of the demonstrations they couldn't get to work. So they were out of a job. That's the main reason they hated us.

But we continued marching and carrying on as though it was the only thing to do, because we couldn't turn back once we started. We used to try and make it to a van they called the Black Marie. A Black Marie was black, and the story goes it was named after a big powerful lady who would get drunk on Saturday, and it would take about four or five police to put her in one of those vans, so they nicknamed them Black Marie. Anyway, it was the wagon that you got to go to jail in. We would try to go to jail because they would keep you overnight, and that way you were protected. They had these speakers in the jail, and they would tell us Martin Luther King was a Communist and he worked for the Germans and he was coming to break peace between the whites and the colored. And when the Klansmen spoke of him, we used to start singing old Negro hymns and stuff like that. And I remember them coming with fire hoses and they would turn the hoses on to get us to stop singing, and we would take the mattresses and put them between us and the hoses to keep the water from hitting us.

But we kept on and on. One day we went up there to the big house where the mayor lived, to march, and this was when we had been marching for a while now, and I remember when we got there the mayor was standing out on the steps and they had National Guards. We figured, well, this is it. Somebody was going to get killed with those soldiers there.

But the mayor said that from that day on, the marches would be protected. If anyone was caught abusing anyone or throwing rocks or anything, they would be arrested. We couldn't believe what we were hearing. When he finished his speech, we clapped our hands and started shouting and carrying on in the streets. The white folks and the Klansmen could not believe this was happening. They ran out as usual to do their thing. The National Guards caught them and put handcuffs on them and took them to jail, and we were startled. We thought we were dreaming. We never thought this would happen—that the white man would go to jail for abusing us. We just couldn't believe this was happening. But we actually saw this with our own eyes. That was the most rejoicing day of my life.

Our friends and relatives would say to us, "What are you doing? Why are you doing these things? You will never be able to walk in the front door of the drugstore. You will never be able to live in a beautiful house beside the white man. It isn't supposed to happen in life."

But our friends and relatives and also the white man didn't understand the way we felt and the way we thought about the situation, which was we didn't care who we sat beside. We didn't care who we lived beside. We didn't care so much about walking in the front door. What we cared about was who are you to tell us what we can and can't do in America, the land of freedom, the land of democracy. That is what we got beat up for. It was as simple as that.

Afterword

I've worked anywhere you could work to get some money. The only decent long job I've had is here in Baltimore; I've been a custodian at Park School going on thirty years. The rest of the jobs were just in and out, here and there. I did marry in North Carolina, but my wife and I divorced. We had a daughter, and she's still in Raleigh, where she's a nurse, doing good. I remarried and got separated, but I have two sons by that wife. My youngest son is in high school, and my oldest one, he went back down South.

I was honored because Park School where I work gave me a yearbook in my name, and a whole page, dedicated especially to me, and they had a big assembly.

One of my brothers works here at the school, too, and the Alumni Council of The Park School made a scholarship fund in our name honoring us for all our years at the school. The scholarship helps kids who live in Baltimore, whatever color they are.

The school gave a big party for my brother and me. They surprised us with a proclamation from the Maryland House of Delegates. It's very official. It declares the scholarship to be the law. Now, the proclamation certificate is up on the wall of the church where my mother is a deacon. She was the first woman deacon of the church. They have a parents-and-child corner there, and they put pictures up when anybody's kid is doing something good. They do that to try and influence the young people and try and help them see what some of the people are doing that come from that area. My brother and I, we're very proud of that.

A Note about This Book

More than four years ago, when my younger daughter was twelve, she heard Leon Tillage address an assembly at The Park School of Baltimore, as he does every year as part of the curriculum. She came home from school and told me about it.

"Leon grew up in the South," she said. "He talked about the olden days. It was awful."

We sat for two hours that afternoon, talking about what Leon Tillage had said. Well before she finished explaining, I felt that this was a story that should be told to more than just the seventh grade at The Park School. It seemed to me the world should be listening to him.

I made an appointment to meet with Leon. I told him how moved my daughter and I had been by his story, and I proposed that he try to tell it to a larger audience in book form. I asked if he would allow me to try to help him. He agreed.

By the next day Leon had spoken his story onto a tape for me. The text for this book was transcribed from that original tape and from two other tapes that were made later for clarification purposes. We have tried very hard to be faithful to and respectful of Leon's own precise voice. All editing was done with his participation and approval. We tried to restrict the changes to bridging the gap between the spoken word and the written word.

In anticipation of making collages for this

book, I read many books, fiction and nonfiction, about the American South in the 1930s, '40s, and '50s. Leon and I also made a pilgrimage to his old home in North Carolina. I saw all the places that he talks about in the text. Many of the buildings are no longer there, but I have walked on the actual ground where they used to be. The house on Mr. Johnson's farm is gone, but Leon was able to show me traces of its foundation, and pieces of the fireplace structure are still there. Providence School is no longer standing either, but I saw an antique potbelly stove in the house of Leon's brother. Together both brothers showed me where the wood used to be placed. I was warmly welcomed by all of Leon's family. I listened to them tell family stories. I studied the family photographs. I took many of my own.

Finally, with the feeling that even one picture would be too many for Leon Walter

Tillage's words, I have chosen designs and patterns as accompaniment for this text. The collages are made with soft black mulberry paper on top of heavy white stock.

What amazes me most about Leon is his prevailing optimism. When I ask him how he can stay as he is, he talks about his parents and his strong religious upbringing. He talks of his parents' strictness, and also of their constant unconditional love, strength, and support. He speaks of his mother's difficult but successful struggle to keep the siblings together after his father's death.

"But, Leon," I've said many times, "you have no bitterness. How come?"

Leon smiles. "What good would that do? I know there were bad times," he says. "But you know, there were rejoicing times, too."

Leon has witnessed major changes for African Americans in his lifetime. By participating in the marches, he himself helped to make these changes happen. This fact alone must contribute to his positive outlook. In telling his story, Leon Tillage is continuing his peaceful protesting by helping to educate people. We all need to know and to remember the history over and over again. We all need to help the changes to continue.

—*Susan L. Roth*